My Dog
A Book About a Special Pet
Heather Feldman

The Rosen Publishing Group's
PowerKids Press™
New York

For Penelope, Dylan Beau, and Kelly

Published in 2000 by The Rosen Publishing Group, Inc.
29 East 21st Street, New York, NY 10010

First Edition

Book design: Danielle Primiceri

Photo Illustrations by: John Bentham

Feldman, Heather L.
    My dog : a book about a special pet / by Heather Feldman.
          p.   cm. — (My world)
    Includes index.
    Summary: A young boy describes what is special about his dog.
    ISBN 0-8239-5524-9 (lib. bdg.)
    1. Dogs—Juvenile literature. 2. Dog owners—Juvenile literature. 3.
Human-animal relationships—Juvenile literature. [1. Dogs. 2. Pets.]
    I. Title. II. Series: Feldman, Heather. My world.
    SF426.5.F45   1998
    636.7—dc21
                                                 98-49397
                                                  CIP
                                                   AC

Manufactured in the United States of America

Contents

This is my dog, Duke.
Duke is a good dog.
Duke knows how to sit.

5

Duke knows
how to shake
hands with
me. Good
boy, Duke!

1

Duke knows how to
play ball with me.
Good boy, Duke!

9

Duke and I have snacks together.

Duke and I take naps
together.

13

Duke walks with me.

Duke even helps me with my homework.

Duke is the best dog in the world. Good boy, Duke!

When I am ready for bed, Duke gets sleepy, too. Good night, Duke.

21

Words to Know

BALL

DOG

HOMEWORK

NAP

SNACK

Here are more books to read about dogs:
Dogs (First Pet Series)
by Kate Petty
Barron's Educational Series

Our Puppies Are Growing (Let's-Read-and-Find-Out Science)
by Carolyn B. Otto, illustrated by Mary Morgan
HarperCollins Children's Books

To learn more about dogs, check out these Web sites:
http://www.geocities.com/Heartland/Estates/1210/

http://petstation.com/dogs.html#top

Index

Word Count: 84

Note to Librarians, Teachers, and Parents

PowerKids Readers are specially designed to get emergent and beginning readers excited about learning to read. Simple stories and concepts are paired with photographs of real kids in real-life situations. Spirited characters and story lines that kids can relate to help readers respond to written language by linking meaning with their own everyday experiences. Sentences are short and simple, employing a basic vocabulary of sight words, as well as new words that describe familiar things and places. Large type, clean design, and photographs corresponding directly to the text all help children to decipher meaning. Features such as a picture glossary and an index help children get the most out of PowerKids Readers. Lists of related books and Web sites encourage kids to explore other sources and to continue the process of learning. With their engaging stories and vivid photo-illustrations, PowerKids Readers inspire children with the interest and confidence to return to these books again and again. It is this rich and rewarding experience of success with language that gives children the opportunity to develop a love of reading and learning that they will carry with them throughout their lives.